Hitchhiking on the Road to Wholeness

For my Thursday Prayer Warriors

And Kristy

I am thankful you are all in my life

All scripture quotes are taken from the *World English Bible*. But please use whatever translation is easiest for you to understand.

CHAPTER ONE

Mirror Mirror

The mirror cracked from side to side
Along with all my hope and pride.
And now my life is out of place
Without a way to see my face.

I do not have great strength of arm,
Or crackling wit or subtle charm,
I'm clumsy as a newborn lamb,
A Nobody is who I am.

Without a face I stumble by,
To find my home beneath the sky.
With nothing to offer, nothing to give;
Still I want a place to live.

I need someone to take my hand
And lead me to a new found land,

Where still waters reflect a face

That doesn't scream of my disgrace.

I am looking at myself in my bathroom mirror. *Really* looking. Not doing a quick check before going out the door or studying only my eyeballs as I take my contacts out at night. I am surveying my entire face, and taking in the rest of me as well. I am pulling back the curtain of denial that I walk around with to keep myself from admitting the truth.

I am ugly. This is the truth I see. No one will ever want me. As soon as I leave the safety net of my parents' home, I will have to be prepared to be alone. I will need to take care of myself, without a partner to care for me.

I don't cry any tears of self-pity. Those have come in plenty before and will probably return to haunt me later. Right now I am facing cold, hard reality and telling myself that I need to get it together and figure out how to proceed with life from here. My secret and somewhat shameful dream that someone will fall madly in love with me and want to be with me for the rest of my life is just that - a dream. One I am too mature to nurture anymore.

It scares me. And shames me too. But I am

filled with a new-found determination to find a fulfilling career and stick with it. This is what I must live for.

If only that feeling was enough to cover the gnawing ache that has now opened in my heart. A sick feeling that says goodbye forever to the innocent joy of childhood. It will shatter my faith in a loving God, affect the rest of my life, and nearly swallow me whole.

Do I bother to question what God himself thinks of my plans and pain? Do I give him a chance to refute my logic or even comfort me?

No. I don't bother. If he made me, then he made me like this. On purpose. He could have made me beautiful. But he didn't. He must have known that I didn't deserve beauty. So I don't talk to him, and therefore get no answer except a loud silence.

Maybe you're here with me. Maybe you have had your own life changing moment of self-discovery in the past. Maybe you are having one right now. It might not be about physical appearance. You might be beautiful (I will try not to hate you) but you think you lack intelligence, or feel you don't have the right social skills or physical abilities. It could be anything related to your self-image. That's the way mirrors lie to you.

And they do lie.

The above story is one hundred percent real. It happened a long time ago, when I was just a teen. I wish I could go back and tell my stupid teenaged self that it was all a lie. That mirrors lie. The world lies. Parents lie. Friends lie. *You*, you stupid idiot looking into the mirror, *you* most definitely lie. You tell yourself you will not let this moment stop you from succeeding in life, you say that looks don't really matter to you and having someone think you are beautiful doesn't really matter and that you are a big, brave girl for facing things so valiantly.

You're a big, big, LIAR.

It matters. It matters so much.

So let's pick up a stone and throw it with all our might at that mirror. Shatter it. Watch it break, pieces cracking and splintering in a thousand directions. Rejoice over its demise. You can no longer see the false image of your lying self.

But now what? Do we go through life without

ever looking in a mirror again? That seems challenging.

We should probably fix it. And anyway, I don't know about you, but part of me wants to know the truth. If the mirror lies, then what exactly is it lying about? There must be a truth to counter the lie. Just fixing the mirror won't change what I see. Somehow, I need to change *how* I see. And I don't think there is an optometrist alive that can fix my eyes. Because it's not an eye problem. It's a soul problem. But I can't fix my soul, can I? There's probably a song or two out there about it, but I don't think just listening to tunes will be enough. I was born this way, right? There's no real fix.

Is there?

Let's leave it for now. Instead let's go on an adventure. One without mirrors or unrealistic dreams or valiant bravery. Just a trip to get to know who we really are. A way to see ourselves somehow without a mirror. A way to maybe find our soul without having to listen to a bunch of country songs.

I say "we" because I don't like to travel alone. It's scary. So unless you put this down and walk away right now; you're coming with me.

Buckle up, buttercup.

Kristy's Questions

This is the part where I ask my good friend and beta reader Kristy to question everything I just wrote. I will try my best to answer.

1. *Why do you think you are a nobody and ugly?*

The answer to this question is easy. I merely measured myself by the standards of the world and found my physical appearance lacking. It was also a time in my life when I had experienced a lot of rejection and wasn't sure why I was so seemingly different from everyone else and therefore unappealing. But I asked God for an answer (we are on speaking terms now) because he can get right to the heart of it. He is smart that way.

"Your enemy, the devil, will always lie to you and tell you that you are not enough. He is the father of lies. Even those the world would say are the most beautiful, the most popular, the smartest, and the richest

still get lied to daily. But I NEVER lie. And I tell you now that you are made in MY image, by me. Don't you dare agree with a lie that says I made something that is not enough. You pleased me from the moment I formed you in your mother's womb. I desired you from before time itself began. Exactly as you are. Man makes mirrors, but I see the soul I created to be with me for eternity. I never tire of looking at you. You are beautiful, inside and out."

(John 8:44, Numbers 23:19, Genesis 1:27, Psalm 139:13&14, 1st Samuel 16:7, Psalm 8:3-5)

2. *Why don't you accept how God made you and find the good in that?*

After reading the above lines I really should. But it's hard to fight the daily reminders of my lack, even if I tell myself they are lies. It will take a journey of faith. But every journey has a starting place, and believing what God has said is a good beginning. So we should go back and read the above lines from God (and the Bible verses) often. Maybe before we even leave this page.

3. *If the mirror lies, how do you know what's truth?*

Good question. I will have to start with believing that the Word of God is truth. You have to start somewhere, and if you can't even go that far I hope you will still hang with me. If there is no truth then there is nothing to base your life on, nothing under your feet at all. You will float away without the truth of gravity, so start by choosing to believe in something, even if it's just that I might make sense eventually. Faith is belief in the evidence of things unseen, isn't it?

Disclaimer:

Never just buy something that someone said when they claim to hear from God or speak for Him. I will always add some references from The Bible to back up what I believe I heard God speak. And I don't take the responsibility of speaking for Him lightly. I wouldn't have the guts to do it at all except for the fact that I need to hear from him and I want to share it with you, so that neither of us must go it alone. I'd like to believe that you need to hear these things too.

I do believe it.

That's faith.

CHAPTER TWO

Creeper van

Nothing

You are allowed to hold: Nothing.

No carry-on items, no checked bags,

Fanny packs, purses, or pocket sags.

Drop it all now if you want to go on.

I mean it.

Naked

Like a newborn babe fresh from the womb.

No ideas about who you are,

A rejected lump or a bright, white star.

We need a starting place.

This is it.

Have you ever been lost? I don't mean a temporary moment where your GPS must re-route you because you turned down the wrong road. I mean bag over your head dumped on a dirt road to nowhere kind of lost. You thought you knew what you were doing but suddenly you are staring down a gravel road with no sign of life in any direction and you don't know exactly how you got here or which way to go? Or kid in the grocery store wandering down the aisle looking for Mom lost?

If you know where you are going in life and never felt that moment of panic like the rest of us experience, then you would be a good companion for me on my hopefully not fruitless journey. You will have advice and be all positive and inspiring and all that.

But I don't want you. I don't want to be given a goal or told to pull myself up by my bootstraps or suffer your condescending pat on the head. Someday, I don't care how smart you are or how rich or how much you have it all together, someday you too will feel lost. Then come back here and you can join me. Until then I only want other desperate souls who might have a chance of understanding what I am going through.

You still there? Still with me?

Alright. Let's do this. Imagine me rubbing my hands together and grinning at you.

Yes, I am still lost. And scared. Terrified really. And I don't know which way to go. But together you and I are going to wait for the next vehicle to come by and stick out our thumbs and start our journey in whatever shows up going wherever it takes us. Sound good?

Not really, I know. But at least we have each other. I promise not to leave you behind.

<u>Please note:</u>

I am not actually suggesting anyone hitchhike in real life. This story is only a metaphor, which means it is symbolic only, used to represent something else. Hitchhiking is crazy as a box of frogs. That saying is also a type of metaphor called a *simile*, and you're welcome for the grammar lesson. Last one, I promise.

Picture it.

We are standing on a country road. No town in sight. We have nothing but the clothes on our backs. I am in ordinary clothes: jeans, a t-shirt, and tennis shoes. You can wear whatever you want, whatever makes you feel comfortable. You are essentially my invisible companion so as long as I know all the essential parts are covered (and in my mind they are - this is not that kind of book) we are good to go.

A slight breeze stirs up the fallen leaves at our feet, like the beginning of a Hallmark movie. The sun beats down. We wait. Contemplate our navels. Try to recall for a moment what we looked like before we smashed our mirror. The image is just a hazy sketch in our minds. And we hated that person, remember?

We hear a rumble in the distance. An engine throbbing in the still air. Maybe some music? We strain our ears... yes, definitely music. Is that the Charlie Brown theme song? We glance at each other and shrug.

Then we see it. A van. A mottled gray van with rust around the edges that suddenly barrels into view. Not a mini-van. An actual van. No back windows. No markings. Instead of being reassuring, the *Peanuts* theme music suddenly gives off a very different vibe. Serial killer-like.

We are about to be kidnapped.

Maybe this whole thing was a bad idea.

The van slows dramatically with a squealing of brakes when the driver catches sight of us. Is it too late to call this whole thing off? Unfortunately, yes. I said we would take the very next ride, so we will. I am clearly insane.

We expect to find several men in black outfits and ski masks jumping out from the back but instead the van comes to a complete stop and the driver waves through the open passenger window in a friendly fashion. And she is a very harmless-looking elderly woman. I scrub my eyes to make sure I am seeing clearly. You probably do the same.

"Good morning!" she shouts above the music. "Need a lift?"

I manage to nod. She gestures towards the van and smiles wide, revealing less teeth than she should have. I turn to you and grab your hand, which feels a little sweaty. I am *so* not doing this alone.

Once we climb into the passenger seat the woman turns off the radio and looks us over. Having no idea how we look anymore I squirm under her assessing gaze. What does she see? Is that pity forming in her milky cataract-filled eyes? Eyes that probably shouldn't be driving? How is it that a half-blind toothless old lady has pity for me?

"All by yourself?" she asks. I nod again, unable to find my voice and unwilling to explain to her about my invisible friend. Is my aloneness the source of her pity? Yet she seems to be alone as well.

"I can take you as far as the nearest town, but then I am going to need the room."

I nod again. She probably thinks I am a mute. I look around the van as she starts to drive. It is filled to bursting with stuff. Twisting to look behind me I gape at the mounds of stuff. All kinds of stuff. Boxes of clothes, old lamps, stuffed teddy bears, broken picture frames and dressers with missing and crooked drawers. Things you might see at a garage sale. In a bad part of town. The dashboard is piled with stuff too, smaller trinkets that look like rejected McDonalds toys. Even my feet have to compete for room with bags of papers and three or four pairs of old boots. It's a good thing your invisible body doesn't take up any space.

"What's with all the stuff?" I blurt out, finally finding my voice.

"I'm a hoarder," she announces bluntly.

"Oh." Her honest confession is startling but somewhat reassuring. Crazy people don't admit their problems like that, do they?

She cocks her head at me. "Aren't you gonna ask me why?"

"Umm, sure, okay. Why are you a hoarder?"

She takes her milky eyes off the road and turns to face me. "Because I never get rid of anything. Even got all my old teeth." She reaches under the seat and grabs a jar of teeth and shoves it in my face. I flinch back, and I hear you make a disgusted sound in your throat. Keep it together over there.

"Why?" The question comes out of me almost without my permission. Do I really want to know?

Her eyes are fortunately back on the road in

front of us but I see the droop in her face. "What you own defines who you are." She is speaking in whispers now, almost talking to herself. "If I get rid of something and I need it later then I would be sorry. I can't trust anyone else to have it for me. I have to keep it. I have to, I have to, I have to."

"It sounds like you need some counseling."

She makes a *pfft* sound. "I tried that. Worked for a while. But when they made me get rid of my stuff I almost died. At least that's what it felt like. I was so hollow, you know. Empty. The stuff makes me feel better. Safe."

"I understand." I really do understand. She feels like I do. But I don't want to end up in an old van surrounded by junk in order to feel okay. There must be a better way.

"Thanks for understanding." She grins, flashing her gums. "It is so nice to have someone to talk to. Nobody wanted to stay with me and my stuff for long."

"Well thanks for picking us, I mean *me*, up."

"No problem. Glad to do it." She starts humming happily to herself, something that sounds like "Winnie the Poo".

There is something sharp digging into my hip and I pull out a headless Barbie doll from under me. I raise my eyebrows at you and toss her onto the floor. The more I try to get comfortable on the hard seat the more stuff I realize is stuffed in the cracks. I find what looks like a rubber rat jammed under the seat belt. As I pull it out, I realize it is not actually made of rubber. It is a real rat. Just a dead one.

I squeal and throw it out the open window. Sanitizer. I need sanitizer. And maybe some Valium.

"What'd you do that for?" the old lady hollers. "I was gonna sell that to a lab."

"I thought *I* was crazy," I mutter to you under my breath. "Next she'll be selling *us* to a lab."

Suddenly she slams on the brakes, throwing us forward into the dashboard. I gasp and rub my bruised sternum. Seat belts, next time. Hopefully rat-less seat belts.

"Sorry." The woman pats my knee. "I really enjoyed having company, but you are taking up too much valuable space." She looks unbearably sad.

"I might find more things on the road. And you might throw more stuff out. Stuff I might need. I can't let you ride anymore."

I climb out quickly, still gripping your hand. I wouldn't leave you in there for all the tea in China, even if you did forget to tell me to buckle up. She would have buried you in stuff she *might* need. Though it seemed to me she needed friends more than stuff.

You and I have no stuff. Only ourselves and our wits (meager) and our experience (limited). But I know I don't want to end up like her. I look at you. Let's make a pact, you and I. No collecting stuff. The only things we are learning will fit in our head and our hearts, hopefully plugging the leak in our souls that keeps us from being happy and whole. We will collect no baggage to weigh us down and keep us from fellow companions we may meet along the road. Deal?

So right now, drop anything you are trying to carry, and I will do the same. In this story we have nothing, and I want to keep it that way. We start from scratch. We don't even have faces. And that is after all, what we are here to find. Our identity.

Our face. Who we truly are and who we wish to be.

Maybe they can be one and the same.

Kristy's Questions

1. *Isn't it safer (and easier) to stay and be the person in the mirror that you hate rather than trying to change?*

Possibly. But settling for that type of existence, the one that says "I don't need anybody, I will just take care of myself" is such an empty and hollow place. We are built to need others, and we are born wanting acceptance. Every story ever written, every religion followed, every human tragedy perpetuated on the earth has its roots in the idea that we *absolutely need* something beyond ourselves. If that person in the mirror can't get that need fulfilled, we need to find a way to change it.

1. *What things are you trying to carry that you need to drop?*

Anything that I hang onto that I think might

fulfill that need. I need to start from scratch so I can do this right. No hair products or make-up to hide my true appearance, no fancy clothing to hide from the elements, no medals or ribbons proclaiming some accomplishments. Just me, naked as the day I was born (only with some clothes because there is no nudity in this book, it's just a metaphor remember). I need to be like Adam and Eve, naked but feeling no shame. (Genesis 2:25)

The shame came later, when their eyes were opened to the knowledge of good and evil. The point here is that the way God made them didn't cause them shame until they sinned. So I need to get back to looking at myself without the shame that I feel because of my worldly knowledge of good and evil. The world says, "Ugly equals evil; Beautiful equals good". Or "Smart equals good", or "Strong equals good". And even if I can wrap my brain around the fact that maybe that's not true, it's hard to get it deep down in my soul, to the part of me that drives all my emotions and actions. So I have to dump everything, because I don't know enough to judge rightly. I need to believe that God does, and through this journey he will help me see correctly. And live free to be me. And you live free to be you.

I can't wait to meet us.

Here's what God has to say: "**There is nothing wrong with enjoying the things of this world. Just keep it in the proper perspective. The only lasting thing that should truly concern you is your soul. It's the only thing you take with you to the afterlife, and the only thing you are responsible for. You can trust me with it. I long to be your comfort and place of safety.**"

(Luke 12:15-34)

Practical Matters

I don't know about you but although I like a good story, I always want to know how to bring the truths home to me. Don't give me just a pretty poem or a fancy tale. Tell me how this affects my life right now. Otherwise it's just entertainment. And that's not enough at this moment because, may I remind you, I currently **have no face.** And I am basically writing this book to find it once and for all, and to have peace with who I am. Hopefully as I drag you along you will be helped too. I really appreciate you coming with me. You're a good person.

But we have some homework to do, my good person. Our assignment for this chapter is to imagine there was a fast-spreading fire coming for your home. You only have time to grab seven items to take with you as you make your escape. Everything else burns. What would you take?

Here's my list, you get some paper and make your own:

1. My purse

2. Photo collage of my family

3. Computer

4. Phone

5. Kindle

6. Favorite old book

7. Another favorite old book

Now whittle it down to just three things:

1. Purse

2. Computer

3. Favorite old book

Notice how the family picture I didn't think I could live without got thrown under the bus? But those photos could be replaced because I have most of them on my computer. Some of them anyway. And that book can't be bought for love or money. Many of the books in my collection are irreplaceable. Arrgh! I can't let them burn! But...do I really need them? Or are they just dead rats?

Now select only one: (Don't panic, you can do it)

1. Computer

Can you live without that one last thing? I'm not sure I can. My computer has all my unpublished writings on it, and photos, and copies of paperwork I absolutely need. It's a lot of my life. Now I must imagine dropping it in the fire that is raging around me. Watch it curl up and turn to ash, vanishing in the wind. Bye bye, years of my life.

I still escape. *We* escape. You did this too, right? You didn't leave me to suffer on my own, did you? I didn't think so. I knew you were the right stuff. So now everything we have has burned, but we are fine. We are free. Those things were nice, but they can no longer hold us down. They don't own *us,* we own *them*. That's freedom and power, baby! Fling out your empty arms and dance about! No fire can hurt us!

I'm so proud of us.

Still feeling a little bereft? The bible says

(Deuteronomy 31:8 & Hebrews 13:5) that God will never leave you or forsake you. He can't burn away, so let his presence comfort you and trust that he will take care of you. It's not too much trouble for him, that's what he wants from us anyway. So when you feel that sense of loss swirling in you, just imagine that God is with you, holding your fire-proof soul in his hands.

"I have held many things in my hands and I have lost them all; but whatever I have placed in God's hands, that I still possess."

Corrie Ten Boom

CHAPTER THREE

Find the line

Nothing to offer, nothing to give.

Do I still need a reason for me to live?

Is purpose in life really just a dream?

Or am I somehow more than I seem?

When I feel broken, without a link,

Can I still become more than I think?

Was I made to fail and be swept aside?

Or in my smile does God truly hide?

The wind is picking up. It's a nice breeze, cool enough to be refreshing but not so cool it makes you shiver. This is good because we have no coat. Just the clothes on our backs, remember? And even those are sort of fixed to us, like clothing sewn on a stuffed animal or doll that can't be removed. I hated those as a kid. I was always annoyed by the inflexibility. But for the purposes of this story, that is how our wardrobe behaves. No costume changes. No flexibility.

And don't start fussing about it. I am the writer and I get to decide how things go, and there is no arguing with me. Yes, I may have just uttered a slightly maniacal mad-scientist chuckle. Don't be scared, after all I am on this journey too so I can't write more than I myself can handle. And I am a huge chicken. No worries there. I just hope you imagined yourself in an outfit that's both good-looking and comfortable, because you're stuck with it now.

We are still alone on the road, walking slowly and trying to figure out why we didn't pick more comfortable shoes when the sound of an approaching engine teases our ears.

Our next ride. Hopefully less weird than the hoarder.

We are pleasantly surprised to see a sports car approaching. A nice one. Most people have a favorite, and feel free to insert your own over mine, but I am seeing a cherry red Ferrari straight out of Magnum P.I. Only the music doesn't match. It's some girly pop song, one that I hate. Well, you can't have everything.

I stick out my thumb and as if on command the car stops with a loud squeal of the brakes. I walk to the door and it swings open dramatically. I almost expect fog to roll out. But as I duck my head inside, I am pleasantly surprised again. While it isn't Tom Selleck it also isn't the old man I was expecting. You know the stereotype, that only old retired guys can afford sports cars. Well, this driver isn't old. He is maybe in his late twenties, early thirties. Prime of life. And he is not wearing a Hawaiian shirt and shorts but a very well-fitting three-piece suit. His dark hair is swooped above his head like a well-jelled awning, and his cheekbones are sharp enough to grate cheese. He looks like a Ken doll.

So probably safe, right? Anyway, this is a made-up story, so it really doesn't matter. I will remind you that hitchhiking in real life is bad juju, even if the guy looks like Mr. Rodgers. But our guy looks like Ken, who also never hurt anybody, except when he jilted Barbie at that beach party. And I made that up when I was eight. So in the Ferrari we go.

Yet before we can climb in our new sweet ride the driver holds up his hand. "Just a moment," he says. Do I detect a slight British accent? It's hard to tell because he doesn't bother to turn down the music, which has now switched to some boy band. But I half expect him to tell me his name is Bond, James Bond.

I pause with my hand on the door. "Yes? Are you not stopping to pick me up?"

The driver turns his head to face us. He has a chin dimple so deep you could keep a goldfish alive in it. But what catches my attention are the mirrored aviator sunglasses he is sporting. I spy my faceless reflection staring back at me. Creepy.

Ken doll speaks. "What do you have to give me?"

"Excuse me?" My reflection's blank-canvas face scrunches in confusion.

"What will you give me as payment for taking you somewhere?"

"Listen, buddy. I don't know what you think is going to happen here. This is a G rated book. And I am no Bond girl."

He laughs. I try not to be offended. "I take cash or credit, honey. A nice watch. Maybe an iPad."

Now I am even more confused. "Hey, I was holding out my thumb. You know, *hitchhiking*. Not hailing a cab."

He smiles and flashes a row of pearly white teeth. "Sweetheart. Everyone has something to offer."

I shake my head, trying not to look over at you. I know you don't have anything either, and I don't want him to think I am even weirder than I look. But what could he mean? Do I look like I am hiding something somewhere on my person? Or does he think I have a balloon of cash somewhere uncomfortable, like a drug mule?

I clear my throat. "I'm sorry. I don't have anything."

He looks me over with a slight sneer. "Clearly.

You should be better prepared in the future. Everyone is looking for something from everyone else. Don't you know that? That's how the world works. You want a ride from me, don't you? Why should I not expect something from you?"

"How about my companionship?" I state that as a question, because he does not really strike me as someone who is lonely like the last lady. It is just a desperate hope.

The handsome eyeless face turns away. "Companionship?" His voice is so quiet I barely hear him. He stares ahead for a minute without moving. "That can't possibly be enough. Is it? Nobody wants just that from *me*." He seems to be speaking to himself, so I hesitate to reply. I obviously want more from him, I want him to drive me away from here.

Then he shakes himself, like a dog after a bath. "You obviously have nothing real to offer." His voice is back to its normal superior tone. "No ride for you today." With that the door jerks out of my hand and closes with a loud click. The car peels away, narrowly missing my foot.

What a jerk.

What does he mean I have nothing real to offer?

The comment stings, reminding me of the reason I am out here wandering down a road with only an imaginary friend (or real-life reader) along for company. I really hate the writer in me right now.

We walk forward again, my feet scuffing the gravel dejectedly. I spy what looks like a quarter on the ground and pounce, only to discover it is just a piece of useless metal. I toss it to the other side of the road in disgust. But as we continue, I find myself looking around, hoping to find something along the roadside worth keeping. Maybe something to offer the next driver. I might get lucky and find a few coins, or even a lost wallet, or maybe a discarded watch. I am the writer, I can put something on the road for me to find. Should I do it? Would it change things? I need to have something to offer. If I had even some junk, maybe the first lady would have let us ride longer with her. Though it wasn't very comfortable in her creeper van.

And we agreed not to take anything.

But I wouldn't pick up junk. Only good stuff. Only I don't know exactly what would be good stuff to the next driver. The old lady was hanging onto a dead rat, but Ken doll would have much higher standards.

And there's the problem. Each person has a different standard of what is junk, and what is an acceptable "something to offer". Unless I can read the mind of the incoming driver ahead of time, there is no way to know. I could just keep everything I find, but then I would have to start carrying dead rats. No way.

The point is the line between what is junk or not is movable. Different for everyone. Therefore it can't be judge-able. It can't be predicted, even if each person thinks it can, based on their own ideas. I could try to find my perfect match based on where our lines met, but what happens if I lose my stuff? Would that person still value me? And what if they lose their stuff? Or their line goes in the wrong direction? Would I have been willing to let Ken doll hang out with us if he didn't have a cherry red Ferrari? Does that make me as big a jerk as him?

Just the thought of all the complications makes my insides squeeze with panic. I need a paper bag to breathe into. I am insecure enough with the whole no face thing. I can't take this on too. It's too hard.

We were right to not take anything. It all had to go. It's the only way to know if we have any value just in ourselves. That's sort of what we are trying to find, right? A face worth seeing? But right now we are back to where we began, without a face anyone would want, and without anything else to offer.

Feels rather bleak. But we have each other, don't we? You are still here with me, aren't you? Please say yes. I have to believe there are others out there who want to find acceptance just because of who they are, not how they look or what they can offer. There must be others who are desperately searching for a truth to hang onto.

That maybe God didn't make a mistake with me.

Or you.

Kristy's Questions

1. *Why did the guy pull over at all if he wasn't willing to give you a ride?*

Maybe he hoped I had something he wanted or needed. Or maybe he really wanted companionship but couldn't admit it to himself. In a world where you are judged by what you have to offer, it is hard not to see others through that lens as well. Don't judge him too harshly. Most people secretly evaluate you all the time; will you be a good friend, a good potential mate, a good worker, etc. He was just more blunt about it. This is why I found my own face unacceptable. I judged it with the lens of the world.

2. *Where are you even planning on going? And what will you do when you get there?*

I wish I knew. It started out as simply running away, but I know I will learn some things about myself along the way. I suppose I am hoping to find some acceptance somewhere. A place to belong, with my old face or my faceless face or a new face.

3. *Why are you faceless?*

Ah. This is where it gets symbolic. Since the face I saw in the mirror was not something I thought anyone would want, I sort of wiped it out in my mind. The mirror broke, so I have no reflection right now. And I am searching for a place where I can get a new face, a better face, or something else equally acceptable to others. (See question 2.)

"I find you exquisite. As unique and beautiful as a snowflake, striking as a sunset, mesmerizing as the falling rain. I made you. For me."

(Genesis 1: 26&31, Zephaniah 3:17, Song of Solomon 7:6)

God, please help me believe that.

Practical Matters

Today's homework assignment: Put away your distractions and spend some time meditating on the fact that you do have things to offer to God. You may have thrown all you own into the fire, but you still have your soul, your body, your time. Even if you couldn't move or speak or even pray, just determining to spend your time with the one who created you is extremely valuable. Just sitting and doing nothing but being with him. Can you do that? Enjoy the fact that he is enjoying being with you, his beloved creation. Breathe in that thought. Breathe out your insecurities and inadequacies. He makes you adequate. *More than adequate* if you believe what he said about you on the last page. Put down your phone, put away this book, and choose to believe.

I'll try it if you will.

CHAPTER FOUR

Denial

Denial is a drug that once you ingest,
Makes life a race without a rest.
You must take a hit every single day,
To keep the ugly reality at bay.
But the truth will haunt you in your dreams
And tear your false self at its seams.
One day you will lay down and die,
If you do not confront the lie.
But to face the truth and find success
Takes courage very few possess.

As a child I remember riding in my parents' station wagon. It had a back seat that faced the rear so you could look out the back window and watch what you just left behind. I loved that sweet ride. I miss it, along with the naive, innocent kid that enjoyed that backwards view.

I see something similar coming at us down the road now. Nostalgia has me back to being young enough to not care very much what I look like or what others think of me. I am happy and free, riding down the road without a care. But that small blip of my past was so short lived it is almost fuzzy in my memory. Did I ever really feel that way? It seems unlikely. Maybe in my childish fantasies. The world and its judgments intrude into life pretty quickly, and innocence is stolen almost before it begins to truly breathe. I remember feeling different and out-of-place very early on in life.

My Brady Bunch moment is still with me though as the green and brown vehicle stops at the sight of my out-stretched thumb. The car is old and the paint is a little worn, but it still looks inviting. Homey-like. This time it will be good, I just know it. I have a good feeling, don't you?

Your silent glare speaks volumes. Just because the ones before this were a bust doesn't mean this one will be. Think positive, my friend.

You are still unimpressed, I see. You think the writer will let us down again. I agree it is possible. I know the writer is a bit messed up. But stay with me, please. I need you. I am Jan Brady in a world of Marshas and I need a friend.

The driver is a pleasant-looking young woman who does indeed remind us a bit of Marsha Brady. She waves us in without fully turning towards us and we climb inside. What else would we do? We are here to get a ride and my feet are tired. Besides, the adventure of the road calls!

You try to dive out the door at the last minute but I grab your hand and hang on tight as the car starts off down the road. I knew you were smart. But I am afraid the only way out of this is to stop reading. And that would make you a giver-upper. And a yellow-bellied chicken. I know you are better than that. It's just a story remember?

The driver had been chatting all the while we have had our silent battle (which I will always win because I am the writer) but she hasn't noticed our lack of attention. She has a nice melodious voice, and she is prattling on about the weather. We nod and agree. Yes, it is a nice day for a ride. The windows are rolled down, and the breeze is warm and gentle.

The station wagon, however, seems to be riding a bit rough. It feels like the tires are unbalanced or something. And when I look closely at the driver I notice she has only one hand on the wheel. Her left hand is tucked at her side, facing the door. The car is clean, there is no junk, and she says nothing about payment, so those are two points in her favor so far. So the car rides a little wobbly. Big hairy deal. And she drives with one hand. Lots of people do that.

So there's a teensy-weensy smell of gas. No problem. Old cars sometimes smell like gas. Or maybe she just fueled up. That has to be it. There's nothing to worry about here.

You are getting all tense again, I can sense it. Maybe by the way you are clawing at my arm. I try to engage the driver in conversation to distract us.

You. I mean distract you. I am not worried at all.

"So, where are we headed?" I ask her.

"Home," she answers. "I am always headed home." Then she turns fully towards us, and my tongue dries up in my mouth. The left side of her face is... sort of hanging off. The skin of her forehead is raw and peeled away right below her hairline. A pouch of flesh dangles from her cheek, and her eye is not there. Not actually missing, it just doesn't seem to focus. Or blink. Like it doesn't work anymore. Her long-sleeved yellow shirt is ripped from her shoulder down to her wrist, the edges streaked with dried blood. I no longer wonder about her hand. I only hope she doesn't decide to show it to us. I have seen enough.

You were right. The writer is one twisted individual.

"Um..." I can't seem to find words in my dry mouth. I swallow. You tug at my arm. I know, I know. I got us here, now I need to get us out. "I think we need to go to a hospital," I finally manage to say.

"Don't be silly." She giggles. Actually giggles. "I am going home. You can come too. There is always room at my house."

I don't like the idea of going where she lives. It

sounds like the Isle of Denial. "I really think you need to go to the hospital," I try again. "You're face… it's not right."

"I'm fine." She waves her hand and the car drifts across the road. "I don't want to talk about me."

"Can you just let us off here?" I squeak. You are nodding furiously next to me, your hold on my arm cutting off the blood supply to my hand.

"Of course I can. But why? You are welcome to come home with me. I am going home. I just can't ever seem to get there." She whispers that last part to herself, a frown marring the good side of her face.

"No, we need to stop. Now." I speak as firmly as possible without actually yelling.

"Okay." Her smile is back in place, and her hand is back on the wheel. She pulls over to the side of the road and stops the car. You are out the door before it evens fully stops. Your self-preservation is admirable.

"Would you please see someone about your face? And probably your hand? You were obviously in an accident." I plead with her one last time through the window as I get out behind you.

"Don't be silly. I was never in an accident." She says it with finality, as if her words can make it true. "I am going home."

"Good luck," I call out as she pulls away. "And good luck to us too. We need it."

As we watch her drive off pity for her tugs at my heart. I know she is a make-believe character, but I know so many like her. People who live in denial of their true condition.

Not me, of course. I was brave and faced the truth when I looked into that mirror. Except I am not sure now what the truth really is. And I am sort of running away right now. I can't face being faceless and I won't admit that I have no way of finding a face, so I am jumping in stranger's cars hoping for a fix. My face isn't hanging off but it is completely gone. I'm not much better off than Marsha.

But going to the hospital is scary. It will hurt. And there will be questions.

Is there even a place where I can find a face? A "Faces Are Us"? "FaceMart"? And what kind of face do I buy? How do I pay for it? We already decided we have nothing to offer anyone.

Am I doomed to wander without a purpose or a home?

This sucks.

I am glad you agree. At least we have each other.

Kristy's Questions

1. *How do you get help for something you're in denial about if you don't know how to go about it or feel like you're a hopeless cause?*

First of all, I don't believe anyone is a hopeless cause. Maybe that's naive of me but if I believed that than I might as well just quit writing this and walk away. Jesus died for everyone, the whole world, even the most hopeless, villainous, nastiest specimens. He must have thought they were worth saving, or he would have put conditions on who he saved, instead of taking on the sins of the whole world. It probably would have been easier on him to only die for the best and brightest. Much less garbage and horror on his shoulders that way. But he didn't hold back, he took it all. Therefore, no hopeless causes.

I think this question is just an excuse anyway. And as far as not knowing how, just admitting it and bringing it out in the open is sometimes all that is needed. And hey, this isn't the stone age. Just google it. Tell someone. Get help. Go on a seemingly useless quest with a friend.

2. *If you do get help maybe it will lead to something worse happening and then what do you do?*

This sounds like yet another excuse to avoid dealing with it. Sure, worse things can happen. But some great stuff can happen too. You could be free. You could find out others are struggling too. And discovering you are not alone is one of the reasons I am writing this. YOU ARE NOT ALONE. We are in this together. Don't forget that. I understand the fear in play here. Why do you think I keep asking you to come with me? No one needs to confront things alone. That's why there are support groups. And the best support group of all is The Trinity: Father, Son, and Holy Spirit. The bible says he (they) is for you and not against you, and that he has plans to give you a hope and a future.

(Romans 8:31, Jeremiah 29:11)

"Fear not my child, for I am with you. Always." (Isaiah 41:10)

Practical Matters

Today's assignment: Come with me to the hospital. I know, you'd rather not. There's nothing wrong with you. You aren't in denial about anything. Well maybe I just need someone to go with me. I already established that I'm a big chicken. You could just sit in that chair next to the table in the exam room and hold my hand. Would you do that? Please?

And maybe if you walk through this with me you will find your own courage and pull your car over and stop being a Marsha.

The doctor comes in to check me over. He doesn't seem too scary. I check his hands for needles or other instruments of doom. Nothing. Maybe this won't be so bad.

He wants to know what I am in denial about. What in my life am I refusing to deal with? I don't really know, that's kind of why I'm here. I know something is wrong, I know I am not happy or free, but I'm not sure why. And I'm not sure I want to know why.

He says I need to take some time and ponder it before he can treat me. That if I am quiet and still it will come to me.

Then he leaves. Wow. Really earning his top dollar.

I sit in silence, squeezing your hand. Anything coming to you? Something is occurring to me, unfortunately. I have a relationship issue. There is someone in my life I am holding things against. I try to forgive, I ask God to help me, but I never seem to get anywhere. I think I don't really want to forgive this person. If I forgive then no one will know how I have suffered. It won't be made right. I deserve better. I shouldn't have to be the one to bend when I wasn't in the wrong. Right?

I can think of a lot of inspirational quotes about the healing of forgiveness, and how unforgiveness only hurts me, blah, blah, blah, etc. But no quote can ease my pain. I want to not feel any more pain and I deal with this person all the time. They aren't going away. And the pain won't stop. Unless I deny it, and then we are right back on the road with half my face hanging off.

The doctor comes back in and smiles at me. He

says he is proud of me for facing my pain. He says he is going to give me some medicine that if I take daily will help me forgive. That seems cool. And way too easy, but hey, I'm no fool. Gimme those pills.

He hands me a bottle that looks like something from "Alice in Wonderland" and has a sign on the neck that reads: "I choose to do what is right".

"Forgiveness is right. It is not to be confused with Justice," he says to me. "And it has nothing to do with being deserving. If it did then God would not forgive us because we really don't deserve it either. He sent his son to take the punishment we deserved and that's not Justice. But His love did it anyway. That's righteousness. We become a little more like him every time we choose to do what is righteous, not what makes us feel vindicated or eases our pain. When you take your medicine, your face will reflect him. God will see to Justice. He will love you *more* than you deserve. You just choose to do right by forgiving and God will do the rest. But you need to take it every day. Every day is new and needs a new dose. But you will need less and less of it as time goes by." He smiles. "I would suggest you take it with food, because it's a bit bitter on the first swig. It gets sweeter once it goes down."

"Okay, doc. That was an impressive speech. I especially like the part about my face reflecting God's. I really needed to hear that. Maybe there is hope for me. Fortunately, I have written your words down so I can refer back to them often. I can be a slow learner, but I will take my medicine. And give me a bottle for my friend here too. I'm sure they have someone they have to do right with." I look at you and wink. "We can make a toast to our success together."

I have to include one inspirational quote. It's one of my favorites.

"Darkness cannot drive out darkness; only light can do that. Hate cannot drive out hate. Only love can do that."

Martin Luther King, Jr.

CHAPTER FIVE

Many faces

Who am I?

A prankster?

A clown?

Good for a laugh?

A sarcastic knife that will cut you in half?

A loner?

A geek?

A target for the weak?

Will I lay down and be a big rug for your feet?

A yes-man, a minion, a follower of kings?

If you ask me will I just become anything?

Will I hold your hand when you are sad?

But never say

If I feel bad.

Do I get to have my own time to cry?

Or will you cut me down if I even try?

Who am I?

A fraud.

A fake.

God’s mistake?

I don’t even know what face to make
Without someone to placate or please.

No one knows the real me.

No one can see.

Not even me.

Have we given up yet? How resilient are we? What will happen if we turn back or simply lie down by the side of the road and give up.

Maybe we need to just walk.

That's it! We should just walk! No more having to risk getting into some lunatic's car. No more finding out how we don't have what it takes, or don't want to have what it takes because it will make us hoarders or deny that we have problems. We don't need a driver. We will drive our own little two-legged vehicle.

Let's do this.

So.

Walking.

It's tons of fun so far.

You could say something, you know. Make some conversation.

How's the weather today? Yup, it looks like rain. Yay. We can walk and get a shower at the same time. Maybe the writer will give us a break and hold back the rain.

You are looking at me funny now. I know I am

the writer, I'm not crazy. Really. Stop looking at me like that! You see I am also a character, and ask any writer, characters have no rights. They live to do the writer's bidding. Therefore the *character me* is walking and hoping the *writer me* won't make it rain. But I know I'm a jerk. The rain is coming.

Let's just keep walking, okay?

Okay.

This is fun.

Walking is *sooo* much fun.

You don't seem to be agreeing with me.

Me neither. I'm pretty stupid right now.

Writer me is about to stop writing this book when we hear the wonderful sounds of an engine approaching. I all but leap into the road, risking life and limb and jerking out my thumb like I'm having a seizure.

Please don't take my eagerness personally. You are a fine companion, just a little on the quiet side, and I am lazy. Besides, we probably won't learn anything by just walking. And now we will use that knowledge and our recent boredom to help us get over the fear that is twisting our insides as we get a good look at the car.

Not that there is anything wrong with it. It's a white four door sedan. No rust, no hood ornaments, no bumper stickers. Nondescript. Nothing alarming there.

But we know better by now. The driver will be a deranged undead zombie who wants to eat our brains. Or maybe a little old lady with a bunch of purse-sized dogs. Could go either way.

The driver stops in a slow and controlled manner. A sudden rumble of thunder in the distance makes us jump. It's now or never. We square our shoulders and get in the car.

You were really brave this time. Good for you.

The driver is an equally nondescript young man who appears to be wearing some sort of Halloween mask depicting the face of Spider Man. Okay. We can deal with this. Maybe he's on his way to rob a bank and we can ride in the getaway car. It will at least get us to the safety of a police station.

"Hi," I say, brilliantly. "Thanks for picking us - I mean me - up."

"No problem," he says, his voice muffled a bit by the mask. "Glad to help."

He steps on the gas and we take off, a little too fast for comfort. We are pressed back into the seat like we are climbing the hill on a roller coaster. There hadn't even been time to put on our seat belts, and I am fumbling in a panic to get it secured. "Whoa! Slow down!" I shout at the driver in a panic.

"Sorry." He instantly slows. The Spidey mask falls off and is replaced so quickly by another I almost didn't see it happen. I blink and rub my eyes. This one is a baby, complete with pacifier and bonnet. He glances at us shyly. "Is this better?" We are now creeping along the road at a snail's pace.

"Yeah. Sure. Thanks." The eye holes in this mask are even smaller than the other and I begin to doubt his ability to see anything properly. Going slow sounds like a good idea. "Are you sure you can drive?"

The words are barely out of my mouth when he executes another lightning-fast mask change. This mask is a police officer. Is this his superpower? It's kinda cool. Scary, but cool. It makes me wonder what he really looks like. Is he scarred or something? Is he the Elephant Man?

"No need to worry, I got this." His voice sounds like he might be winking, but it's hard to tell under the mask. "Where are you headed?"

"Nowhere really."

"Oh, just cruising? Going where the wind blows?" Now the mask is of some sort of dreadlocked hippie in a beanie. I swear I didn't even see that one change.

"Actually... I'm sort of on a quest-type thing. Trying to find myself."

"Really?" I can see his real brows scrunching up under the hippie mask. I am kind of surprised this one stayed on this long. "Why? Isn't it easier to just be what everyone wants you to be?"

Now I understand him. Maybe better than he understands himself. "Can you do me a favor?"

"Sure," he says. This request seems to make him comfortable again. I am willing to bet he is used to people asking things of him. But he won't like what I am going to say.

"Will you let me see your face? Your real face?"

He stops the car. “Why? Why would you want to see that?” He is looking down at the floor, the mask trembling over his face.

“I’m curious.” I lean over and touch his shoulder, feeling a pinch of sympathy in my chest. “I’ll bet it’s a nice face.”

He says nothing for a minute. The only sound is the humming of the engine and our nervous breathing. Then he turns and slowly removes the mask.

He is not scarred by burns or deformed. He is not the Elephant Man. We were prepared for that. We were not prepared for this.

He is faceless.

I practically jump over you to get out the door.

I am a terrible person. You might be too because you didn’t stop me.

We just left him. We ran away. It hit too close to home and we ran away. No wonder he wears masks. For some reason he hates his face just like we do and his only identity comes from wearing the mask of whatever he thinks others want of him.

We really are awful. We finally found someone like us and we ran away.

We are the Cowardly Lion.

But I refuse to wear a mask. There's some courage in that, isn't there?

Kristy's Questions

1. *Where are we going again? Can't we just rest awhile?*

According to chapter 1, we are trying to find ourselves. Or a face to wear, or maybe we are just running so we don't have to face our facelessness. It's morphed a bit, based on the people we have met and our own weariness. And I am weary too, okay? God promised me that this book would be short because he is not interested in drawing out our agony or making us earn our answers. But he also knows our stubborn nature, and that we must learn by experience. Hence the hitchhiking, even if it's metaphorical. I promise we are near the end. Hang in there. Go get a cup of coffee or take a break and come back if you need to. I will be here waiting for you, just like God.

2. *Why did you have to see his face to begin with?*

Really? Human nature, baby. Maybe you are some superhuman who doesn't peek at their gifts under the Christmas tree but even though I like surprises I still had to know. You know? If you didn't care what was under the mask, then I didn't do my job as a writer very well and I apologize.

3. *Why would you run away? Maybe you could search for a face together?*

I never claimed to be courageous. And YOU, reader, are my chosen companion. I need someone willing to be without a face, not someone who just wears masks. That is not an answer, and it is exhausting. Keeping all those masks and changing them out at a moment's notice? Nope, can't do that anymore. And we would be exposed eventually. We need someone who will give us a face that is acceptable to everyone, or at least to the few who might be worth caring about. Onward!

Or go take your break. Whatever.

"Beloved, the need to be acceptable to everyone is a needless burden. Please set it

down and remember that you are acceptable to me. I made you. My death and resurrection made you acceptable in every way, removing the barriers of your helpless imperfections so we can be together without guilt or the need to please. You please me by just allowing me into your life. Come to me and learn to rest and enjoy who you are and what we have."

(Matthew 11:28-30, Acts 10:15)

We all know people who claim to be always true to themselves. They feel the need to make sure (usually loudly and often) that we know where they stand on political and religious issues, to the point where they are uncomfortable to be around unless you agree with everything they believe in. They often use their philosophy of "being themselves" as an excuse for rude or even unkind behavior. Don't be like them. That's the first assignment.

But neither should you have to change who you are and how you speak or act around different people to the point of changing your personality or keeping part of who you are under wraps. That's not freedom. Free to be who we are is not the same as not caring about how we affect others. We can be ourselves and still be courteous and kind. Unless you are a psychopath. I know you aren't, or you wouldn't be reading this.

For today I want you to be mindful of how you are acting around others. Do you just react to what they say or how they act? Do you fake feelings you don't have (or deny ones you do have) to avoid stirring up the waters? Keep a journal for the next few days and record your thoughts.

Also pay attention to how accepting you are of others, especially those who differ from you. Do you judge them, even secretly? Be honest with yourself.

And at the end of this book I will record my own journal experience. I won't make you go it alone.

CHAPTER SIX
We walk alone

There's a hero in my vision.
A strong one in my dreams.
The romantic cowboy riding off
Never again to be seen.
The one who, knocked down, keeps getting up.
The teeth gritting underdog
With all the scars and stuff.
The one who needs no one and carries on alone,
Who says "Bring it on"
Through every broken bone.
He always has the knowledge,
He always has the strength,
He will reach the goal in sight,
He will go to any length.

There's a hero in my vision
Who will finally make me free.
The strong one with no lacking,

Someone I long to be.

My face won't mar

This movie star

This hope to which I cling.

The loneliness a melody

Which all the stars will sing.

I will have no need for anyone

When this hero comes to be.

The only heartbreak comes then

When I know it can't be me.

Okay.

Sitting by the side of the road waiting to die seems like a good plan. At least we're together, right?

You don't look so happy. You're not thinking of ditching me, are you? I know I have not led us well so far, but don't give up on me yet. Don't put the book down and walk away. Please. I swear it will have a happy ending. (At least I hope so, otherwise, what's the point?)

But hey, no one murdered us. Or took us to rob a bank or made us hold a dead rat for more than thirty seconds. Those things should count for something.

But I agree with your silent plea. No more hitchhiking. We're done. Finished. Kaput.

But still faceless.

And this gravel is digging into my butt.

Alright, let's try walking again. I know it's tedious but at least we will be moving. Thankfully you are still here and agree with me and we get up with a renewed determination. And no arguing because if the writer says we are determined then we are determined.

We round the bend, hand in hand. (Too much? Okay, forget the hand holding.) We round the bend (not holding hands) in the road and see a sign. And I don't mean metaphorically. I mean an actual sign; big, neon, and garish.

"SMITTY'S USED CARS - GREAT BARGAINS!

SOMETHING FOR EVERYONE - 1/4 MILE AHEAD!"

Maybe this is the answer! We can buy our own car and take ourselves where we need to go! In excitement we race ahead. Turns out neither of us can sprint for a full quarter mile (the you in my mind is non-athletic, like me) and we end up walking the last bit, huffing and puffing. We top a hill that nearly kills us and then suddenly there it is in all its grandeur: Smitty's Used Car Lot. It's a cracked parking lot full of mismatched junkers and a small, decrepit shack with a broken sign that reads: Smitty's sed ars.

It's not as nice as we'd hoped. But it suits our budget since we actually have no money. And there are plenty of different vehicles in various states of rust here so there must be something for us. I hope Smitty will take a check. A fake check.

The man who emerges from the shack is not what we anticipated. I expected a loud suit, slick-backed hair and maybe a paunch. This guy looks like a high school math teacher from an 80's film. He has thick glasses, a receding hairline, a scrawny frame and tan slacks. He's even wearing a sweater vest.

I feel the need to study for a pop quiz.

"Hello!" he calls out in a friendly voice. "Looking for a car today?"

"Well yes, we are. You must be Smitty."

We shake hands and he smiles at us. "That's me. Alrighty then. No sales pitch here. You can have anything that you can drive away." He gestures at the lot. "After you pass the test, of course."

I knew it. He *is* a math teacher. "What kind of test?" I glance at you nervously. I hope you remember your high school algebra. Because I don't.

Smitty's smile is reassuring. "A simple driving test. Each vehicle has one attached to the key. Pass the test and the key will turn. Good luck!" With that he turns around and disappears back into his shack. Probably to grade papers. Or watch Oprah.

This seems oddly simple, but maybe the writer is finally taking pity on us. We start surveying the lot, looking for the best car. Small would be good, something with good gas mileage. We don't have stuff so no need for storage. You spot a powder blue two door in fairly good condition. Good job. Glad I brought you along.

Inside there is a sheet of paper hanging from the key.

"To drive this car, you must be able to stand on your head, unassisted, for ten minutes. Then complete one hundred sit-ups, fifty push-ups, and seventy-five jumping jacks all while reciting the lyrics to *The Star Spangled Banner*. Backwards."

This seems insane. I'm pretty sure I can't stand on my head for ten seconds, let alone ten minutes, and as for the other stuff... remember me saying I was non-athletic? Somehow I thought the test would be about, I don't know, driving a car?

I look at you and you look back. Yeah, I didn't

like this car either.

We select a different one, only to find a similar test attached to the key. Only this one involves quadratic equations and diagraming sentences while jogging in place for an hour. We begin to get suspicious.

And yes, after an exhaustive search of the lot, we confirm that every car has its own form of torture as the only means to get a key to turn. And yes, we also tried to cheat and just turn the keys without completing the tests, with no success. So now you are not only my companion on a seemingly hopeless quest but also a cheater. Sorry, I just couldn't go down alone. And you know you wanted me to.

Finally, we pick what we both agree is the easiest test and try to finish it. All we have to do is prick our finger on the needle attached to the key and spell out the ABC's in blood on a piece of paper. This was an automatic no-go the first time we saw it basically because I don't like needles or pain or blood not to mention who else might have used that needle. Hello hepatitis. But now it seems easiest. I even volunteer my finger. Only we discover that fingers don't bleed as easily as they do on TV. It takes all my fingers, and we are only on the letter E. I am wondering if using my toes would be considered cheating when a buzzer sounds and a robotic voice announces that we are out of time. We are timed too, huh? This system is rigged.

So we try a different test.

And fail again.

And try a yet another one.

And fail.

I sense a pattern here.

Tired, sore, bleeding and dispirited, we trudge to the shack and pound on the door. "Smitty! Open up!"

He pokes his bespectacled head out. "Yes?"

"These tests… I mean, they're ridiculous."

"Really?"

"Yes! No one could do them!"

"Yet people have," Smitty retorts. We don't appreciate his sudden sarcasm. What happened to the friendly teacher? Now he is more of a snotty lunch lady.

Then an idea occurs to me. "Maybe the tests were really just tests. To sort of prove we would be willing to try." I look at him hopefully. "Well, we tried. We tried *a lot*."

Smitty chuckles at that. "The tests were just tests," he repeats in a mocking tone. "That's a good one. Haven't heard that one yet."

I nod, hoping he isn't really laughing at me. "Like in The Karate Kid, when all that work built up the kid's muscles so he could do the moves." I do what I think is an impressive karate chop in the air. You seem impressed at least. "We tried lots of tests, Mr. Smitty. We must have built some muscles."

He looks us over critically. "I don't see any."

That's the last straw. "Look here, skinny." I poke a finger in his bony chest, barely cushioned by the sweater. Who does he think he is, insulting us like this? (I think you look way more muscular, by the way.) "I'd like to see you pass those tests."

"I don't have to. I'm Smitty." He looks down at my finger like I dipped it in fecal matter. Kinda wish I had. "If you can't pass a test, you can't have a car. Those are the rules. I can't help you any more than that." The door is shut in our face.

It only takes a moment for my anger to fade and the similar ache of hopelessness to swamp me. I don't want the mirror to be right. That can't be the end of the quest. I was promised a happy ending! But I was right to think no one would want me, wasn't I? I can't even get a junker car from a stupid guy named Smitty. I don't know why you are still hanging around me, honestly.

I'll give it one more chapter and then I'm done.

Kristy's Questions

1. *What is it all for anyhow?*

Well, I am trying to get some answers. Maybe? Trying to get somewhere in life. Possibly? Trying to figure out how to *do* life. Or just running away from the fact that I don't like myself but either don't know how to change or don't really want to change. I looked into the mirror and didn't like what I saw. But I can't afford plastic surgery. And I don't want it. I want to be okay with who I am, but I don't know how. And just taking care of myself seems so lonely. And scary.

2. *It doesn't seem like you're getting anywhere.*

True. But that's not technically a question. Apparently, Kristy is as frustrated as I am with this whole thing. But hang on, there's just one chapter to go. Okay, one chapter and an epilogue. But that's it, I swear.

3. *Why not just give up and settle for what you have?*

Because I don't like what I have. I am unhappy with who I am and where I am. And I stubbornly refuse to settle for this. There has got to be something better. And I want to help all the others out there who feel the same way. Because I also refuse to believe that I am alone.

"I am grieved when my people refuse to believe in grace. They think they must earn my love and approval, and they in turn demand others be deserving of their own love. Grace is undeserved, and a free gift. Yet you throw it back in my face. If you want to be free to love others without hindrance, to be free of unforgiveness and hate, you must first accept my love completely as it is given, without cost or condition. I love and died for even those who will never accept me or receive the gift of my love. Make my heart swell today by believing that these words are trustworthy

and true, and they are for *you*."

(1st John 4:18&19, Numbers 23:19, Ephesians 2:8&9)

I want you to visualize something with me. Clear your mind, and maybe your immediate environment, of distractions. There is nothing else you need to do or think about right now. In fact, you need this time. It is a matter of survival. There is nothing more important than this time, this moment, right now.

Take a deep breath. Now picture yourself looking in the mirror. Apologize to yourself for not liking something about who you see. Tell yourself that you are God's creation. Not a mistake. There is no need to add, subtract, or improve on anything. Even if you never move from this spot and never do anything good for anyone ever again you are worth the suffering and death of Jesus. Imagine the whip striking his back. That was for you. He took it without complaint or back talk because he was thinking of you. Yes, *you*. He wanted you to know him and be with him so badly he took every lash, every strike with fists and words, every rejection and humiliation. Willingly.

You were worth it. So apologize for thinking otherwise. Forgive God and forgive yourself. Say it out loud. Repeat it daily if you need to. I do. I have verses taped to my mirror to remind me of these things.

You don't have to be Mother Teresa or Martin Luther King or Billy Graham to be worth the price Jesus paid. You don't have to have the bible memorized or have the right family or even be religious at all. If you could earn it then he wouldn't have had to die, he could have just made it some kind of contest and given the prize to the deserving. But the bible says, "For God so loved the world, that he gave his one and only Son, that whosoever believes in him should not perish, but have eternal life." (John 3:16) Jesus Christ is the great equalizer. He made us all different just like the flowers are different colors and the animals are different breeds. He shows his creativity and his desire to have a family, not a bunch of clones or robots that look and act the same. But he treats us all the same. Loves us equally. No need to earn his love and no way to fail it.

Accept it already. There is no greater freedom to be found.

CHAPTER SEVEN

The lie

Is anything ever too good to be true?

An endless summer?

A bottomless cup?

A mountaintop high that only goes up?

Would you recognize it if it appeared?

Or would you scoff or flee?

Would you say yes to one who loved you enough

To come on bended knee?

I know of someone who would qualify,

Who would take you as you are.

Who wouldn't insist you change at all;

Who would only ask that you answer the call.

A teacher, a lover, a friend in need;

A savior in white on a prancing steed.

One to be true

When you are false,

One who will rescue

When you are lost.

Who will say "I love you" right out of the blue.

Yes, friend, that one

Is too good

To not

Be true

To you.

Despair is a heavy overcoat on a sunny day. A nagging bureaucrat who keeps telling you that you haven't filled out the forms correctly. A dripping faucet that...

Alright, stop poking me. Getting poetic is just my coping mechanism. You know we need to find a way to cope. Something real that isn't dead rats or perfectly formed cheekbones or the right mask. And I refuse to live in denial. The fact of the matter is that we are trudging down a road with no hope in sight. We have lost the plot and even the writer is sick to death of us.

Then our ears here the sound of an engine. It does not help though. We have given up on hitching a ride to the stars. The price is too great. To weird. To wrong.

Though there is a different sound to this engine. It's loud, purring in our ears like a caress. It feels like a knock that comes to your door when you're tired and don't want to get up, yet you feel a tingle of hope that the person on the other side will be worth the effort of rising from your chair. It's also coming from the opposite direction.

It's a motorcycle. This is encouraging at first

because everything is out on the open on a motorcycle, no hiding your crazies. But this is a motorcycle unlike any I have ever seen before. It's white. Not off-white or cream or even a dirty white, but pure, blinding white. More pure than fresh falling snow, or a movie star's teeth. Way more pure than the white sedan we hitched in earlier. It almost hurts our eyes.

We both turn fully to watch it approach and get a good look at the man riding it. He is wearing ordinary jeans, a plain brown leather jacket and sparkling white tennis shoes. It is just as inconceivable that he can keep those shoes so clean and pure as the unbelievable white of the motorcycle. As he slows down and parks next to us he removes his full-face helmet to reveal a mane of brown hair, and deep, peaceful dark eyes. He smiles and it is so dazzling I am momentarily speechless.

"I will take you where you need to be," he says.

I look back at you. Are you up for one more try? If I promise this is it? The last one? You nod, though I sense your reluctance. Our luck has been epically bad. And it will be a tight squeeze to get both of our butts on the back of that bike. But something about his eyes pulls me in, as if he can see my soul and is still okay with it. And I know you sense it too.

"We don't have any helmets." I spout the only objection I can think of.

"Don't be afraid." The man speaks with utter confidence. "You can wear mine." He hands it over, somehow pulling one out of thin air for you too. Does he actually see you? He must, if he is offering you a helmet. This is a twist I didn't expect.

"Okay." I shrug, slipping on the helmet and getting on the bike behind him. You get on behind me and we take off. It doesn't feel nearly as weird as I thought it would. His back is a strong wall of confidence and warmth, and I feel light and free as we speed down the road. I reach back to squeeze your hand where it rests around my waist, and the kinship we have is as if we were family. The sense of acceptance and oneness brings tears to my eyes. I think we finally found the right ride.

Then, rather abruptly, he slows and stops.

"What are we doing?" I ask.

"Stopping for a rest," he answers, letting the

kickstand down with a sound of finality.

"But you said you would take me where I need to go!" I know I sound whiny, but he really had my hopes up for a moment there.

"I said I would take you where you needed to *be*. And that's with me." He holds out his hand to me expectantly. "And right now I thought we could have a picnic."

I look behind him and there off the side of the road is a valley of soft-looking grass and flowers surrounded by tall trees, their branches swaying gently in the breeze, beckoning me. I take his hand and swing my leg off the bike, noting the strength of his grip, and how safe it makes me feel. As we walk down into the valley, I see a red and white checked blanket spread on the ground, with a big picnic basket on it. My stomach growls at the possibility of food. It's been a while since I ate anything, and suddenly I am ravenous.

I practically run down the hill, feeling a little bit like I'm on *Little House on The Prairie,* only pausing to make sure you are following. Once we reach the picnic site our driver opens the basket and all of my favorite foods burst out, and for a while we just stuff ourselves. Eventually I realize I am enjoying myself for the first time since I started this journey. The sun feels warm on my face, my belly is satisfied, and I am not alone anymore.

Our driver has been silent this whole time, watching us stuff our faces like an indulgent parent, occasionally helping himself to the bounty. Now he meets my eyes, and I blink at the intensity there. "You must understand that you don't need to go anywhere or do anything to be whole. I already did everything needed to make you perfect in my sight. You only need to accept and believe it."

I sit up, alert despite the blood being sent to my digestive tract. "So, you're God then."

He laughs, and it is a musical sound. "Yes. Not what you expected, huh?"

"Well, I thought either big, thunder-and-lighting-crabby-old-man-scary or pretty-unicorn-glittery. Though your bike is rather pretty."

"My way is pure, so my ride is also pure. But remember that I made people in my own image, and while my enemies may find me justifiably scary, my children don't need to. They just need to stop trying to take the wheel and let me drive."

You elbow me in the side, and I know you have questions too. "But I don't like myself. How can I be made in the image of God if what I see in the mirror is ugly? The mirror told me that I would never be enough, so I have to take care of myself. I have to have the right stuff, or the right mask, or the ability to not care that I don't."

"And how did taking care of yourself work out?"

"Not well," I admitted. "I've made friends," (I nudge you) "but I am weary. It's hard work, and I'm not good at it."

"You weren't made to take care of yourself. You were made for me. I wanted you. I want to care for you. I will give you acceptance and rest. That is my promise. But of course you have to believe it."

"It sounds too good to be true."

"Yes, I understand. You are more used to people like Smitty, who expect you to earn it. Though while riding with me is free, it will not be all sunshine and unicorns. I want all of my children to ride with me, and many are struggling just like you. I would like you to help them. That's where I'm going today, actually. Up ahead a station wagon has broken down, and a woman sits at the wheel refusing all help because to admit she needs help would be to admit something is wrong and she can't face that. I want to tow her along until she has the courage to face it. It will help if she has a friend with her, someone she already knows."

I know he is speaking of Marsha. But I'm scared too. I don't know him that well, I don't know if I want to see Marsha and her ripped up face again. I hesitate and he waits patiently. The wind blows, and the sun beats down. You are uncharacteristically silent. The writer is no help either. Finally, I stir up enough courage to say what's really stopping me. "I'm no good. You screwed up with me. I can't help anyone."

"Those are a lie."

"Wait, don't you mean those are *lies*? You're God, you should really get your grammar straight."

He gives me his dazzling smile again. "Yes, those are certainly all lies. But they are all really THE lie."

"Okay, now I'm confused. What is THE lie?"

"THE lie is the basis for all the others. It is the womb from which all lies are birthed. If you can stop believing in Santa Claus and the Tooth Fairy and that people mean it when they say they are 'fine', then you can also stop believing in the big lie. Then all others will fall away."

"This is a big deal, huh?"

"Very."

I'm not sure I'm ready for such a profound moment and he pauses, almost asking my permission to continue. You poke my shoulder in either impatience or annoyance, probably both. We came all this way, right? Why wouldn't I want the answer?

Because I am scared. I can't go back to being innocent after this. I will be responsible for what I hear. Still, after grabbing your hand, I give him a shaky nod.

He places his large hand on both of ours. "THE lie that is the mother of all lies is this: that *I am not enough.*"

That's it? It seems too easy an answer.

"Think hard about it," he says. "If I am enough then you no longer need to fill your life with stuff to comfort you. You no longer need to be used to find affection. You do not need to deny your pain to survive, or become what others want to be accepted. And you do not need to find someone else to love you. I love you. My love is enough. It is trustworthy."

"Is it? Really?"

"Test it and see. Come ride with me."

I turn to look at you. Well? What do you say? We were in this together from the beginning. Shall we ride?

CHAPTER EIGHT

Epilogue

I know I left you hanging. But in my mind, I imagine you whispering in my ear, or maybe shouting "Let's ride!" and pumping your fist in the air. Because that's what I'm going to do, and I don't want to leave you behind. It would break my heart. Yet the choice is really yours. Even the all-powerful writer can't make it for you. So please carefully consider everything that has been said so far and then abandon reason and go with your gut. Take the hand of the "Too Good To Be True Man" and climb aboard. His name is Jesus, and he has been waiting to take you to places you've never even dreamed of. The ride will be bumpy, and windy, and at times cold and wet. But you will never be alone.

Now about your face. You and I have one task left. We know Jesus doesn't care how we appear, but he does want us to be *whole*. We can't be whole without a face. So come with me one more time, all the way back to the beginning.

We are back standing in front of that smashed mirror. Pieces of glass surround us, and the thought of having to fix what we (I guess just I) broke is daunting, to say the least. But Jesus said we are loved, and I want to see the face of someone who is loved like that. And his words will help us.

At our feet we see stones. And these stones were used to smash the glass. They have writing on them. Picking one up, we read the words.

"I need to take care of myself, for no one else will."

According to Jesus, this is a lie. So, what is the truth, the antidote, so to speak, for the lie?

Jesus said that he would take care of me. I can trust in him.

As we speak this truth aloud the writing changes on the stone in our hand. It now reflects the truth we have chosen. On sudden impulse, we bend down and use the stone in our hand to pick up a shard of the mirror. It sticks, like a magnet, and we are able to replace the shard in the mirror frame without risk of cutting ourselves. I know this is Jesus at work. Not only does he provide us with the antidote for the lies, he also makes a way for us to heal without cutting ourselves on the lies. So we can stop being afraid that healing will be unbearably painful. I hope Marsha is watching this, because this is what she needs to see. We get to be partakers in our restoration, which I appreciate, but we don't have to be cut to achieve it. Do you get this? Jesus won't just wave a wand and magically heal us, we must choose it, and be willing to follow through, but he gives us all the help we need. And the courage. Because he is with us. He stands at the door and knocks, patiently waiting for us to open the door and ask for him to be with us. He doesn't penalize us for our fear or leave in a huff or ask for a payment. And he could barge in and demand we accept him, after all it's for our own good. But he doesn't. He waits, loving us all the while, not ashamed to be outside our door while he awaits the joy of the day we let him in. What an amazing God!

We are excited now that we know what to do, and we hurriedly scan the ground for the other stones. We amass a collection and one by one, together, we pick up the lies and speak the antidote, changing the lie to truth.

"No one will love us if we don't have something to offer."

Big fat lie. Let's blast this one.

Jesus loved us before we were born. Before we did anything of value. He made us because he wanted us. Our life itself is valuable.

Love that. On to the next one.

"We need to change to please people if we want to be accepted."

I am eager to dump the masks. Let's do it.

God formed us the way we are. He doesn't make mistakes. He loves us just as

we are.

I am sensing a pattern here.

"We need to be strong and able to take care of ourselves."

This lie is especially painful for me. Because I know how weak I am, how weary, and how scared.

Jesus will care for me. He is God, he is capable of being strong when I am weak. He doesn't look down on weakness, but delights to save. He will never leave me.

There are probably other lies floating out there, but I didn't want this book to be lengthy and overwhelming. You get the idea. Jesus is the way, the truth, and the life. The answer to every lie. It seems too good to be true, but yet here we are, facing a complete mirror. Our face is still the same, but if I look closely, I can see the eyes are different. They are the deep brown eyes that looked straight into my soul by the side of the road. And the mouth is the same one that told me I was valuable, and loved. And there is a sparkle there, and light behind my skin that wasn't there before. I don't see the imperfections and the things I need to change. I see someone who is loved.

And the coolest part is that you are right next to me. I have Jesus now, so I am never alone, but having you with me has meant the world to me. And I am completely serious. Thank you for coming with me, for listening to me and putting up with me. We are made for each other, and Jesus does not want or expect us to go it alone. Remember that I am here for you. I am praying over every word written, asking God to help you and make it real for you too. You are valuable, not just to him, but to me. I mean it partner; I could not and would not have done this without you. You are loved. Believe it.

Now let's get on that bike and ride!

Kristin's Questions

I wrote this book first and foremost for myself, so I am going to ask God a few questions this time.

1. What do I do when the old image from the mirror haunts me?

"Remember that I love you. I want you. I value you. Just as you are. Tell it to yourself and choose it. Over and over if necessary. The more you train your brain to choose and believe the less likely those old images will affect you."

2. How do I know what you say is true?

"Read my word. I died for you, my beloved. I encouraged you to write this book because I wanted to tell you these things. And I gave you my heart to share

them with others because you are not alone."

3. How about when I need human physical or emotional confirmation?

"I will send you people that I can love you through. Even a brief encounter can help if you learn to look for them and see me in them. I am loving you through this book. I am the God of the Universe. Trust me to provide what you need."

"God created man in his own image. In God's image he created him; male and female he created them." (Genesis 1:27)

"God saw everything that he had made, and behold, it was very good." (Genesis 1:31)

Do you hear that, my reader and faithful friend? We are made in the image of God himself, and he thinks we are VERY GOOD.

The end.

You made it!

CHAPTER NINE
Journal entries

Day 1

I got my feelings hurt today. Something was said about me that is untrue and I immediately wanted to defend myself. Of course, it's easier to be bold when replying to a text. I know if I was face to face with this person, I would swallow my outrage and not respond. I love/hate that about myself. It is sometimes a good thing and sometimes not. I need to find my center in God's love today so I know how to respond properly. I can't trust my own feelings. Sometimes things need to be addressed and sometimes they should just be let go. I realize, even as I am writing this, that this time I should let it go. It doesn't matter what this person thinks of me, it's only an opinion. As long as I have done what God asked of me in this situation, I am vindicated in his eyes. God's opinion is all that matters. I will rest in that and let my need to have this person's good opinion go. I drop it now, smash it under my feet. Bye, bye. God is doubly pleased that I look to him and let it go. I will bask in that for a while, letting it soothe my

hurt feelings.

It feels nice.

Day 2

Today I felt like a complete failure. Like Charlie Brown, everything I touched was ruined. I know I shouldn't feel this way; it's not really reality. Everything can't be my fault. Other people helped the ruination of life today. But I always take it all on myself. I make everything my fault. I realize now that this attitude is a mask I wear. If I am to blame for everything, I can just clean up the mess and punish myself and I never have to deal with what caused the issues in the first place. It's a form of denial. I hate confrontation so if I take the blame and the consequences, I never have to risk upsetting someone. Or getting them upset with me, which is worse. I want to be liked so badly I will allow myself to always be at fault for everything, and then there is peace. Except it's not peace. I am no better than Marsha, going around with my wounds thinking I'm fine. And I stand in between other people and God, claiming I am some sort of messiah and I can take on their sins as well as my own. How dare I? I think I can carry everyone else's cross as well as my own? No wonder I end up on the side of the road in misery.

I hate people who blame everyone else for their problems and constantly deflect to protect themselves, but my doing the opposite is just as destructive. I need to take this mask off. Now. Today. No more cleaning up after everyone else. I deal with my own mess only. And ask for help when I need it. My God will not deny me help if I ask.

So I will.

Day 3

I hate that I care so much what people think. It has stopped me so many times from doing or saying what I truly want to. Not that people need my opinion on things, there is too much opinion and not enough action it seems like these days, but I don't want to be afraid to act. Sometimes I can overcome it, like when I took time to comfort a neighbor in a setting that could have been awkward and misinterpreted by the group around me. But she was crying and that's a trigger for me. I have to comfort someone who's crying, regardless of how I feel about that person. But more often than not, I am hampered by my own insecurities and hold back when I wish I had the bravery to act.

God, I know I should want to please you above all things, and if that were true in my life then I would not hold back to protect myself. If I see a need, or an injustice, I would act, not look away and say it's not my problem. But my greatest desire is to have a peaceful and comfortable life and not be hurt by anything. There's the honest truth. So I ask you Father God, save me from myself. Please. Make my heart's desire to please you above all things, and then grant me my heart's desire. So I may never turn away again, so I may be your hands and feet in a hurting world. So I may love others, and love you, more than I love myself. Only you can do this in me, Jesus.

Amen.

Up in Wisconsin is where I live,
Homeschooling advice I am happy to give.
And though I despise winter's cruel freeze,
I have enjoyed a lot of great cheese.
Four awesome kids have come out of me;
Of cats I have owned, there have been three.
Gardening and reading I do enjoy,
In board games much luck I can employ.
And while my hubby works for a living wage,
I get to chase characters around the page.
(Thanks, beloved)

If you enjoyed this book, were helped by it, or just read it through to the end without chucking it across the room; please consider leaving a review on Amazon. Reviews greatly help independent authors like me get noticed. Sharing this book with a friend or anyone who would be helped by it would also make me extremely happy.

Hope to see you on the road!

Visit my author page for more books: https://www.amazon.com/Kristin-Dewane/e/B07KX78XTM

www.ingramcontent.com/pod-product-compliance
Lightning Source LLC
LaVergne TN
LVHW031344150826
845673LV00009B/2854

* 9 7 9 8 6 6 3 6 6 2 1 6 1 *